MW00578509

Sinking and Resurfacing

Poetic Reflections on

Being Human

Taylor Wray

INSPIREBYTES
OMNI MEDIA

Sinking and Resurfacing

Distributed globally with Expanded Distribution by KDP. Cover artwork by Frances Vail.

ISBN Paperback: 978-1-953445-12-4
ISBN E-Book: 978-1-953445-13-1
Library of Congress Control Number: 2021944436

 INSPIREBYTES OMNI MEDIA

Inspirebytes Omni Media LLC
PO Box 988
Wilmette, IL 60091

For more information, please visit inspirebytes.com.

To those who find the poetry
in the small moments

Introduction

As I write this introduction in July of 2021, the world is still reeling from the effects of a devastating global pandemic. COVID-19 changed our lives in ways we could never have imagined, leaving in its path worldwide fear, turmoil, loss, and grief. Confronted with a terrifying virus spreading rapidly around the globe, we did what we had to do to try to keep ourselves and our families safe: We began to limit our exposure to other people and to the outside world.

As businesses and schools closed and social gatherings dried up and disappeared, we quite literally retreated into our homes and, in many ways, ourselves. Without the external distractions and constant hum of our "normal" lives, we were left to sit with our thoughts and feelings—our very humanness.

It perhaps seems natural, then, that this collection of poems also turns inward. Whereas my first poetry collection, *Waiting for the Moon*, focused on nature, reflecting my experience of the world around us, *Sinking and Resurfacing* primarily reflects my experience of the world *within* us.

To be clear, this is not a collection of poetry about the pandemic. Certain poems were written during and influenced by the events of the past year and a half, but for the most part the poems in this book were written before that time.

What this book *is* about, I think, is what it means to be human—or at least what it is like to experience being human. To experience joy and heartbreak, hope and regret, wonder and disillusionment—the frequently magnificent and always messy panoply of thoughts and feelings that make us who we are.

For me, these thoughts and feelings often crystallize in brief but palpable moments: perhaps a sudden pang of midnight nostalgia, a feeling of gratitude for something as simple as the smell of home cooking, the haunting recognition of past failures, or the rush of exhilaration in the promise that a new dawn brings. Sometimes heavy, sometimes buoying, they are the moments we experience when that outside hum is quiet, when we are alone with ourselves. These are the moments that, in a stitched-together patchwork, make up a life.

My hope is that the short poems contained in this collection manage to capture something of those moments—something relatable and real and, ultimately, very human.

TMW
July 2021

A Note on Form

Are the poems in *Sinking and Resurfacing* considered haiku? I'll be coy here and say: it depends on whom you ask. They are perhaps more accurately categorized as senryū, a Japanese form of poetry that is very similar to haiku, but which focuses on the human experience rather than the natural world. On the other hand, many definitions of senryū indicate that it tends to be ironic or darkly comedic in tone, and most of the poems in this collection do not fall into that category.

What I can say is simply that I have composed these poems using a three-line, seventeen-syllable structure (with five syllables in the first and third lines and seven in the second) that has been traditionally used in both haiku and senryū. I hope that the form conveys the essence of what I have tried to capture in each poem, whichever category it may rightfully fall under.

Inner Worlds

In five-seven-five
I frame the verse, in search of
A new way to see

Our better instincts
Never quite aligning with
Our hearts' desires

Floating in amber
Golden-toned, honey-lit dreams
As the sun rises

Rows of names and years
Stories told in patina—
The whispers of leaves

Soft rain at midnight—
Always changing the ending,
Rewriting the past

Before you, naked,
Ink-stained and open-hearted,
Spilling drops of hope

Not quite ripped, but frayed—
Another calendar page
As the year goes on

Vows made in the dark
Stumble blinking and naked
Into morning's light

Artful sabotage
Of his own best intentions
A well-polished craft

Following the cracks
Tracing each from end to end
Cataloging flaws—
An oft-visited atlas
Of roads with lost beginnings

*Note: This is an example of a tanka, another
Japanese form of short poem. Tanka are
composed of five lines, traditionally written using
five syllables in the first and third lines and seven
in the rest.*

Oily stains of shame
Settled deep in the fabric—
Lingering shadows

Vices have voices—
Mellifluous by moonlight,
Cold and shrill at dawn

Thirty-eight slow breaths—
Meditative metronomes
Whisper me to sleep

Counting to twenty—
Wearily washing away
Yet another day

Snowflakes and sad songs
Mingle among the streetlights—
I take the long way

In the tree-light glow
Trying to remember when
Belief was easy

Memories & Hope

We live our stories
Seeking a backspace, but find
The past's been printed

On the year's third day,
Awakening to bright visions
Of a new future

Sunlit memories
Crackle through the dark distance
Like gramophone ghosts

Our fortunes are found
In unknowable truths of
Atoms in motion

Like storm-strewn flotsam
Sinking and resurfacing,
Splintered memories

All those lost midnights—
I can still taste them, the burn
Of such cold comfort

Through the darkest night
We look to lengthening days—
New hope's radiance

We itch for the new—
To be uprooted, seeking
Unfamiliar soil

Hope skitters, limping,
Damaged but unswayed, borne on
These delicate wings

We long to belong,
To find our right place, even
Within our own skin

Searching for solace
In fragments of memories—
Soft, sun-faded dreams

Such a fine vintage,
Those mouth-filling, ripe-fruit days,
Our bold, ruby youth

Useless photos of
Impossibly azure seas,
Well-thumbed memories

Late winter's gray light,
Slush-bound and weary, dreaming
Of a new season

Rare are the moments
When, on quiet wings, we fly
Above the wild world

A new day rises
As we do, born from shadows,
Stretching toward the sun

Wandering among
Twilit streets, wisps of the past—
Faded mannequins

Looking back now
At the halfway point
And still so much to learn

Connections

We share but slivers
Of our unredacted selves—
Careful curators

This beautiful mess—
Our jumbled-up, ragged-edged,
Glued-together lives

The pulsing, humming
Virtual reality
Of words strung just so

Would that we could find
Some latent magic, waiting
To be disinterred

How easily bruised
The silken leaves and soft bloom
Of a tender heart

Through rough, dark currents
We tumble and bob, scanning
For hope's safe harbor

In this raw tangle
Of sinew and bone and skin
We find poetry

Floating in the murk
Between monsters' footsteps and
Dawn's sanctuary

We crave connection—
Someone who knows all our notes
Before we sing them

The quiet magic
Of in-betweens and not-yets—
In the becoming

This writhing muscle
Thumping, hot with bravado—
Just a fragile heart

Warm notes of laughter
As I pass an open door,
The sidewalk empty

Simple Pleasures

Muddled thoughts swept clean
In the snow-swaddled quiet
Of a new morning

We eat in silence
Awaiting the new day's song—
Morning overture

Ashes to ashes—
Finding grace in longer days
And first blooms' promise

Mint tea and slippers
Murmurs of page-turn whispers
A quiet house dreams

The warmth of spices
Cumin, cardamom, ginger
Singing quietly

The pink blush of dusk
Luring me to reverie—
Releasing the day

The old sentinel,
Flecks of gray marking the years,
Still keeping his watch

Forsythias bloom
In yellow revelation—
A world still thriving

Red-eyed Spanish queens
Plunge into a Sapphire sea,
Briny, brisk, and bold

For just a moment
This arcing expanse of stars
Shoulders our burdens

Lockdown gray mornings
Drift, unmoored, one to the next
Lost among the weeks—
Rescued by the smell of rain
As spring slips through the window

Note: See page 21 for an explanation of tanka.

Powerful magic
In a child's expectant eyes—
Wanting to believe

Two a.m. rhythms—
Rooftop raindrops and hushed breaths,
The soft hum of night

A cold rush of wind—
The old dog reconsiders
His snowy exit

Acknowledgements

I once again owe a huge debt of gratitude to Martina Faulkner, who, in addition to being my publisher, continues to be a guide, a cheerleader, a critical eye, and a friend. I thank her for her vision, her support, and her commitment to making the world a more positive, creative, and beautiful place.

About the Author

As a Nashville-born transplant to Rochester, New York, Taylor Wray has found short-form poetry to be the perfect antidote to the long, cold winters. Writing his own brand of haiku and senryū, he creates snapshots of his observations, thoughts, and feelings, 17 syllables at a time.

Join Taylor Wray online: @inthreelines